3.99
BIO
N   32

LONDON
IN OLD PHOTOGRAPHS

DAVE RANDLE
FROM THE JUDGES POSTCARD ARCHIVE COLLECTION

SUTTON PUBLISHING

Sutton Publishing Limited
Phoenix Mill · Thrupp · Stroud
Gloucestershire · GL5 2BU

First published 2003

Copyright © Dave Randle, 2003

British Library Cataloguing in Publication Data
A catalogue record for this book is available from
the British Library.

ISBN 0-7509-3384-4

Typeset in 11/13.5 Sabon.
Typesetting and origination by
Sutton Publishing Limited.
Printed and bound in England by
J.H. Haynes & Co. Ltd, Sparkford.

Introduction

London is not a place you can be indifferent about. You either love it or hate it – or, like most of us, both in roughly equal measure. Beauty and ugliness, horror and glory, saintliness and skulduggery – this capital of kingdoms and commonwealth is as potent a mix of all of these as human art can brew. Whatever you can find, good or bad, in any gathering of our kind is here writ large. And, what's more, as the historical centre of lawgiving and imperial power for much of the world, at least some cultural element of every member of such a gathering can be traced back to here.

Its own existence can be traced to the earliest settlers in these islands. A safe distance up a navigable river whose mouth faced the mainland of Europe, the location was both a haven and an ideal launching point. As far as can be proven by archaeology, London as we know it was founded by the Romans after AD43, although its name is of Celtic origin and probably referred to a home or farmstead already in existence at or near the lowest crossing point on the Thames. The river then spread across the valley and was much shallower than it is now that it has been contained by man-made walls and embankments.

The first 'Londinium' was short-lived, however. Archetypal British battleaxe, Boadicea (or Boudicca) objected to the Roman occupation in the strongest possible terms by burning the town to the ground in AD60. The size and ferocity of her army as it marched on London from the direction of East Anglia were a sure sign something was amiss, so the then governor, Suetonius Paulinus, was able to evacuate the dignitaries and the majority of the other residents, though many ordinary Britons were massacred in the attack.

The rebuilding was soon in hand and this time the fortifications and precautions took account of this experience. Monumental city walls were constructed with lookout towers, sturdy gates and drawbridges, and these were to be retained and developed for the next thousand and more years, their existence immortalised in present-day London place names.

After AD60 the Roman city grew to the north of the river from the fortified 'barbican' at Cripplegate. A wooden bridge was constructed, slightly to the east of the present London Bridge, and waterborne ferries operated at various points, causing development to also begin to the south of the river. There was a governor's palace roughly where Cannon Street station now stands and another substantial Roman palace at Southwark – whose name means 'southward development'. There were temples to Isis and Mithras and one to Diana on Ludgate Hill – now the site of St Paul's Cathedral.

But there was also Christianity in London from an early date. There was a Bishop of London from around AD300 – nearly three centuries before the Emperor Honorius gave up trying to fight off all the Picts, Scots, Irish and Britons who continually besieged him from the north and west, and decided to leave them to it.

By that time the Roman Empire was imploding on all fronts and its influence was soon expunged from the life of the town – although its coinage continued to be used for some time, and trade links forged in its time persisted, despite the general decline of the so-called Dark Ages.

The Saxons were the next major influence on the area, establishing Lundenwic slightly to the west of the old Roman centre. Roughly where Charing Cross and Fleet Street are today, this settlement was more concerned with peaceful local trade with the surrounding kingdoms than with the intercontinental commerce of the Romans. London's traditional markets grew from these sixth-century beginnings.

London had lapsed back into paganism by then, and though there were attempts by Rome to re-establish Christianity they met with little success and it finally centred its efforts on Canterbury. The next Bishop of London was installed in 675.

In the mid-ninth century the Viking sea-raids started, and by 870 there were Vikings in London. But in 878 all were united under Alfred the Great. Lundenwic went into decline as a new settlement grew again to the east. It is commemorated in the name given to a later development in the area – The Aldwych, or 'old wic'.

Now London developed in earnest so that by the time of the Norman Conquest its abbeys, its churches and many of its important public and administrative buildings were already in place. The Normans built plenty of their own but, unlike earlier arrivals, had neither the will nor the necessity to start from scratch. It was under the Normans that London, which was until then merely the most important of a number of administrative centres, such as York and Canterbury, became confirmed as the capital city of England. Removed from the jurisdiction of the counties, it was answerable only to the Crown. Thus its role as a stage for centuries of royal pageantry was also established. William the Conqueror built the Tower of London and his successors built, or rebuilt, most of London's greater or lesser ecclesiastical buildings.

Throughout medieval times the city grew and developed. Every important event in English and British history affected its fabric and its people, but from Norman times onward its personality was formed, its outline developed. It was an organism now with a life of its own, whose right to guide the destinies – political, commercial, temporal and spiritual – of the people of England was beyond question and was now enshrined in perpetuity in the statutes and laws proceeding from it. From then on, even should power devolve elsewhere, it would only be on London's say-so.

Through the second millennium London continued to grow – the Tudors, the Stuarts, the Georgians, the Victorians, right down to our own time a process of change and expansion goes on – some good, some bad. Much has been gained, much lost, but London retains today more reminders than anywhere in the realm of the great civilisations and the just as powerful barbarisms that have helped form our present culture.

Just about everyone visits London at some time in their life. These visitors, like Londoners themselves, partake in the unique atmosphere of the place – share something of the space and time of those who have inhabited its broad squares and its mean alleyways.

This first selection of London images from the Judges Postcards archive will be nostalgic for many. Covering most of the twentieth century, it recalls not only times past, but also buildings lost in the blitz, and activities ended by the advent of television or commercial change. But all of them are redolent of that intangible atmosphere which exists only in London, even though the smog has gone (along with the totters' carts, and the police boxes and the news theatres and the Lyons Corner Houses), and which anyone who has ever been there can identify.

I've enjoyed experiencing it again as I have relived my own love-hate memories of London. It is a privilege to be able to share it through the pages of this book.

LONDON

IN OLD PHOTOGRAPHS

Designed in only ten days by Sir Joseph Paxton, the Crystal Palace was the magnificent centrepiece of the Great Exhibition in Hyde Park in 1851.

Around six and a quarter million people visited the exhibition before the 'Palace' was dismantled and moved to the park that now perpetuates its name at Sydenham Hill. John Logie Baird's television company operated four studios here in the mid-1930s, using the tower as a transmitter, and it was the venue for the first British Motor Show. The football club that bears its name was formed in 1861 and was one of fifteen teams that took part in the first FA Challenge Cup in 1872. The Crystal Palace itself was lost in the fire of 30 November 1936.

Marble Arch before the First World War. London's first tram service ran from here in 1860. Designed by the wonderfully named Francis Train, the slightly elevated lines, which ran along Bayswater Road to Paddington, were deemed to be such a nuisance to all other road users that they were torn up and the scheme abandoned.

Marble Arch before the Second World War. Designed by John Nash as a triumphal entrance and erected in 1827, it is based on the Arch of Constantine in Rome and originally stood in front of Buckingham Palace. The statue of George IV in Trafalgar Square was to have been placed on top. Instead, the arch was removed to its current site in 1851 without George and in 1908 was marooned on an island and ceased to be an entrance to anything, triumphal or otherwise.

Hyde Park Corner in 1909. The congestion charge is still ninety years in the future; the last public execution at what was formerly Tyburn, a mere hundred and sixteen years in the past. Decimus Burton's Cumberland Gate was renamed following the Duke's victory at Culloden. When it was built in 1828 it was known as Tyburn Gate.

The name Rotten Row is a corruption of Route du Roi – the original royal bridleway across Hyde Park, established by William III – and typical of the Londoner's practice of deflating anyone or anything that put on airs.

For generations, parks such as Hyde Park have been known as London's 'lungs'. More especially in the days before the introduction of smokeless zones, they were a refuge from the smog and choking vapours of the city streets. Here, a half century before televisions became commonplace, Londoners gather en masse to take the air on a balmy Sunday evening.

Opposite: Described on the label of this photograph as 'Orators' Corner', Speakers' Corner in Hyde Park was originally the preferred venue for duels. By the nineteenth century cold steel had given way to verbal thrust and parry. This orator has the benefit of an impressive-looking podium. Most used more makeshift stages, often made from old soapboxes – originating the metaphor that an opinionated person is always on his or her soapbox.

The most modern and luxurious hotel in Europe – the newly opened Dorchester Hotel in the early 1930s. Built on land that for seven hundred odd years was part of the Convent of Westminster, it took its name from the mansion built there in 1751 by Joseph Damer, later created Earl of Dorchester. A hundred years on a second Dorchester house, based on the Villa Farnese in Rome, was built in its place for industrialist Robert Stayner Holford, and it was this building that was demolished by McAlpine to make way for the splendid new hotel, which opened its doors in April 1931.

Sir George Frampton's statue of Peter Pan was voted London's best statue in 1921 by a big margin. This photograph was taken soon after its public unveiling in 1912. There is a memorial to Frampton in the crypt of St Paul's.

The 180-foot-high Albert Memorial was officially unveiled in 1876, though it had been completed four years earlier. Prince Albert is depicted reading a tome most people assume to be the bible. It is in fact one of the catalogues for the Great Exhibition – of which there were four of similar proportions, to cover the 13,000 exhibits. The memorial stands next to the original site of the exhibition and its Crystal Palace.

The 6,000-seat Albert Hall was opened in 1871. It cost £200,000 to build, but much of the outlay was recouped immediately by selling boxes in permanence to wealthy concert-goers at £500 and £1,000 a time.

George III moved into what had been the Duke of Buckingham's house in 1762. When it was settled on Queen Charlotte, it came to be known as The Queen's House and only acquired its present name following the remodelling and reconstruction undertaken by John Nash in 1836. When George IV took it over he thought, 'I'm never going to read all these books,' so transferred 120,000 volumes to the British Museum.

Without the television and with a strict embargo on news from the front, military engagements overseas were much more distant than they are today. It was accordingly easier for governments to win the propaganda battle. Captured trophies such as these field guns displayed at Buckingham Palace helped to give some sense of reality to those on the home front.

The Mall in the 1970s. It has already become a bit of a free for all between age old ceremony and the day to day doings of the capital. Taxis and tourist buses just allow enough room for the soldiers to hold their formation.

Trooping the Colour derives from the old military practice of displaying the flag to a troop of fighting men, so that they knew who they were fighting for – or, at least, in less literate times, they could recognise which direction they were fighting in. The annual spectacle incorporates this and the Mounting of the Queen's Guard and has marked the official birthday of the sovereign since 1748.

The Trooping of the Colour takes place on Horse Guards Parade. The Horse Guards building stands opposite the old War Office and is guarded by members of the Life Guards. It was designed by William Kent in the middle of the eighteenth century.

Below: Now one of London's main shopping streets, Regent Street was designed as a single project by John Nash in 1813, though much of it has since been rebuilt. Nash's grand design involved stylish colonnades on some stretches of the street which, while they helped to keep pedestrians dry, created an almost perpetual darkness, so they were removed again in 1848. This picture shows a scene typical of this bustling thoroughfare in the late 1930s.

This is Oxford Street just before the First World War. In the nineteenth century it had been variously known as Acton Road, Uxbridge Road, Oxford Road and Tyburn Road. St Ivel cheese and Black & White whisky were well-known brands being promoted on what were then still London 'General' buses.

Below: Clarendon House, described by Samuel Pepys as 'the finest pile I ever did see in my life', stood on the present site of Piccadilly in the seventeenth century, but it was demolished in 1683 by a syndicate of rich developers and bankers who, according to John Evelyn, wanted to build a 'new town, as it were, and a most magnificent piazza'. The revue *On With The Dance* had recently finished a run of 229 performances at the Pavilion Theatre when this picture was taken. The biggest song in the show was 'Tea for Two' by Vincent Youmans.

Piccadilly Circus in 1909. The figure of Eros was the largest aluminium statue in the world. Designed by Sir Alfred Gilbert and put in place fifteen years before this picture was taken, it was removed to the Embankment Gardens between 1923 and 1929, during a major reworking of Piccadilly Circus, and spent the Second World War in Egham.

Below: Londoners and visitors gather for the first time at the Cenotaph in Whitehall in 1920. Its designer, the great Sir Edwin Lutyens, intentionally omitted overt religious references from its elegantly simple design, so that it could act as a focus for all races and creeds.

Whitehall after the Second World War.
More wreaths, more dead to remember.
Lutyens' Cenotaph is not just the symbol
for a city, but for a nation, a kingdom
and a commonwealth. Once a year its
image – and its meaning – is beamed all
over the world through the medium of
television. Not merely a monument, it is
an ever-present reminder to the
politicians down the road.

The old motto of the BBC was 'Nation shall speak peace unto nation', and this is where they said – and continue to say – their piece from. Bush House is the centrepiece of The Aldwych, where it faces Kingsway, and has been the home of the BBC World Service since 1940. Aldwych means 'old town' and refers to the rookeries and garrets swept away here by these wide new streets in 1905. This photo was taken shortly after the commissioning of the new building.

This is the Strand immediately after the Second World War. The streets are once more
thronging with pedestrians – many of them in demob suits. Drink and chocolate are
back on the menu according to the advertising posters.

Opposite: Bush House from the Strand side. As its name suggests, the Strand was
originally on the riverfront. It was once notorious for its decaying and treacherous
condition. Edward III introduced taxes to pay for its improvement and quite a wide area
of land to the south of it was reclaimed from the Thames.

Perhaps London's best-known landmark, it is understandable that Tower Bridge is often mistaken for London Bridge. The mechanism that lifts the opening sections is powered by huge underground generators. Although each weighs more than 1,000 tons, they can be raised in under two minutes.

When the cargo ships offloaded their freight at London's docks and wharves, anything that wasn't going on up river by lighter or barge would be distributed by carters such as these gathered on Tower Hill.

Opposite: In the early years of the twentieth century the Thames was very much a working river, so Tower Bridge was called upon to make way for fairly substantial craft – hence the altitude of the walkway. Prior to the bridge's opening in 1894, the river was crossed here by a subway tunnel, which briefly contained the first underground railway in London. Operated by cables and steam engines, it was not a success, so all the mechanisms were removed and it became a pedestrian subway. One million people a year used it between 1870 and the opening of the bridge.

Jellied eels from the Thames and eel pie were Londoners' favourite delicacies for around a hundred years, a love affair that began in Victorian times. Dutch fishermen brought their expertise and their boats across the North Sea to capitalise on this demand. With increasing industrial pollution of the city and its river, eel stocks dwindled by the 1940s and the legendary pie and mash shops turned to minced beef as a substitute. Modern day pie and mash shops often serve steak pies with an eel sauce as a nod to tradition. Eel stocks are now largely restored in the river.

Tower Bridge in about 1910. This is a clear demonstration of the boon to the people of the East End, the Docks and Bermondsey of having a road bridge this far down the river. A mere fifteen years after its opening, it is thronged with carts and buses, pedestrians and cyclists.

At first glance there are a remarkable number of similarities between these two views of the Tower of London, taken more than thirty years apart. But by the time of the second one the optimism and economic stability of the 'never had it so good' 1960s had led to the first change in the skyline since Wyatt's Trinity House was built in 1795. Another half century on and this first nondescript high rise is lost in a forest of similarly unedifying edifices.

Although constructed in its familiar form by order of the Norman William the Conqueror, the Tower of London incorporated a large section of the existing Roman city wall. There are suggestions, in Shakespeare and elsewhere, that some form of Tower pre-dated the Norman one – even that it was the work of Julius Caesar. Either way, William's intent was to focus the minds of Londoners on the might of the Normans, just outside their city. The Byward Tower was the first to be constructed on the moated island. Its name comes from the fact that a password – or 'byword' – had to be given before entry could be gained.

Pageants of one kind or another have been popular features of the life of the Thames across the centuries. Here, the latest thing in warships is being shown off in the summer of 1909. And, as usual in those days before anyone worried too much about insurance, every owner of a water taxi or rowing boat is making a few bob by offering onlookers trips to get a closer view.

Opposite: A Beefeater – or, more properly, Yeoman Warder – looks out at Tower Bridge. London Zoo had its origins at the Tower of London, when its Lion Tower was used to house exotic animals gifted to the Crown by the Kings of Morocco and Senegal. When the Tower's last inmate, Rudolf Hess, heard that the famous Ceremony of the Keys had continued uninterrupted throughout the blitz, he reputedly said: 'Now I know we will never defeat you.'

The *Cutty Sark* was the fastest and greatest of the 'tea clippers', though she carried cargoes of all kinds from coal to wool, and travelled around the world many times in her eighty-year seagoing career. Launched at Dumbarton at the end of 1869, she came to rest in the Thames in 1938, following sixteen years as a training ship at Falmouth. Since 1949 she has been dry docked at Greenwich and is now a museum.

Known the world over for the time meridian that established and regulated common time, Greenwich was the birthplace of Henry VIII, Queen Elizabeth I and Mary, Queen of Scots.

The Royal Naval Hospital was designed by Sir Christopher Wren in 1694 at the instigation of Queen Mary II, and was originally known as King William's Building. Admiral Lord Horatio Nelson's body lay in state here for three days in 1806 before being buried at St Paul's.

A typical London wharf.

Opposite: London Bridge in 1912, when the banks of the Thames were lined with
wharves and warehouses to service the steam ships and barges that still came this far
up river.

In this view from the bridge, the extent of river-borne activity in those early years can be clearly seen. Little wonder the capital's air quality was so bad that one of its major causes of death was respiratory disease.

The original London Bridge had shops and other buildings on it in the manner of the Ponte Vecchio in Florence. Even after these dangerous structures were removed the old bridge continued to be treacherous and in constant need of repair, giving rise to the nursery rhyme. In 1789 Ben Jonson described it as a 'pernicious structure', claiming that it had cost more by far in repairs and loss of life than would the building of a new bridge. He went on to say: 'Had an alderman or turtle been lost there, the nuisance would have been long removed.' Nothing much changes. The new bridge, seen here in the 1920s, opened in the summer of 1831. It was designed by John Rennie and widened in 1902. In 1970 it was sold to Lake Havasu City in Arizona and replaced with the current bridge in 1973.

Opposite: Looking towards Southwark, a forest of derricks and a maze of drifting pontoons contributed sights and sounds to the river that were part of everyone's perception of London life. Now they are gone forever.

The Church of St Mary Overie stood at the southern end of London Bridge before there
was a bridge. That – and not what you were thinking – is the origin of its name:
St Mary of the ferry. In 1540 it became St Saviour's as a result of the combination of
several smaller parishes. From 1905 onwards it has been Southwark Cathedral.

The Embankment was completed in 1870. Built on land reclaimed from the river, its tree-lined promenade was designed by Joseph Bazalgette to conceal London's then brand-new sewage main. The big white building is Shell-Mex House, previously the 800-room Cecil Hotel – then (1886) the largest in Europe. The thirteen-storey façade was remodelled for the oil company by Joseph in the art deco style in 1930, not long before this photograph was taken.

The *Discovery* is the ship on which Captain Scott made his first expedition to the Antarctic in 1901–4. It was moored in the Thames between 1937 and 1979, during which time it fulfilled the role of a training vessel for the Scouts. By the 1970s it formed part of a display of historic vessels on the river, but was handed over to the Maritime Trust at last and relocated to Dundee.

Below: A lone artist displays his work on the Embankment in around 1910. When the only other person in sight took a photograph of him, he probably called it a day.

One of the two magnificent sphinxes that flank Cleopatra's Needle, photographed in the 1950s. The 'needle' is actually too old to have been Cleopatra's and, though it used to be described as a gift from Egypt, it actually came from the occupying Turks. It took sixty years to transport it to its present location. It had to be abandoned in a storm in the Bay of Biscay, but was recovered. Beneath its 60-foot-high column is one of the first 'time capsules' – items and clippings from the time in 1879 when it was placed on the Embankment.

The practice of exhibiting trophies of war has been a feature of London throughout history. This photograph shows something that was a real curiosity for sightseers at the end of the First World War – a captured German U-boat, or submarine. I've been able to discover that this is U-151, which was built at the Flensburger shipyards in 1916 and was commissioned in 1917. In its short career – a little over a year at sea – its three patrol commanders succeeded in sinking sixty-six ships, not including naval warships. Its last commander, Ferdinand Studt, surrendered it on 24 November 1918. It was exhibited at various locations around the country before being broken up at Morecambe in 1922.

Nearly sixty years before the guitar-laden 'Waterloo Sunset' was a hit for Muswell Hill's
The Kinks, here's a more smog-laden one from before the First World War. The cranes
and gantries are on the land now occupied by the Royal Festival Hall and probably
served the goods yard for Waterloo station.

An epic building in Oxford Street, frequently voted London's favourite store, Selfridges
– opened in 1909 – also played a vital role in the history of broadcasting. The BBC's
first station, 2LO, began by broadcasting from its roof in 1922.

Swan & Edgar's department store in Piccadilly Circus in the 1960s. There is a line in Gilbert and Sullivan's *Princess Ida* about the unlikelihood of Swan 'seceding' from Edgar, so well known was the store in the early years of the twentieth century, but it happened, and the old place is now Tower Records.

Opposite: The first Harrods store was an existing grocery shop in the Brompton Road taken over by the family in 1849. When the son of the family took over he began stocking quality items of all sorts from food to furniture, originating the idea of a luxury department store. In 1901, now a limited company, Harrods transferred to its present premises in Knightsbridge and, by the next year, employed the best part of 2,000 staff.

Two shots of Carnaby Street in the 'swinging sixties'. This was the hub of the fashion scene and the place for the happening and the groovy to happen and groove. British was where it was at – music, movies, Mini cars and miniskirts. Everything was cool and getting cooler. No one can remember why it all went wrong.

The gateway to St Bartholomew the Great in Smithfield has changed hardly at all since it was built in 1595, although its half-timbered front was for a time covered in tiles designed to make it look like a 'modern' brick building. A bomb dropped from a Zeppelin in 1916 blew them all off again revealing the original façade, which was then restored with the addition of the dormer, new windows and the niche for the statue of St Bart. In 1930 it was condemned. But in 1932 – not long before the earlier picture (above left) – it was again restored and the wrought-iron gate added. By the time the picture on the right was taken – around 1971 – the building on the right had also let a bit more light in on the upper floors.

Rahere was a courtier in the time of Henry I. On a visit to Rome he got so ill with malaria that he swore, if he survived, he would do good things for the needy and infirm in London on his return. True to his word, he set about establishing the basis of St Bartholomew's. Far from lording it as the instigator and major landowner, he occupied himself in contemplation and a life of monastic dedication.

Universally known as 'Bart's', St Bartholomew's Hospital was the more corporeal manifestation of Rahere's promise on returning from Rome. Founded in 1123, it was in the vanguard of medical knowledge right up to the present day. Its position at Smithfield, where country met town, made it an ideal situation for public meetings. Wat Tyler drew something of a crowd here in 1381, when he was leading the Peasants' Revolt. These pictures, all taken around 1910, convey the sense of space and tranquillity that must have aided patients' recovery since Rahere's time. Rahere himself died in 1144.

London's Law Courts were designed by G.E. Street and built between 1868 and 1882.
They were intended to be light pink in colour – the shade of the stone with which they were
built – but years of exposure to city pollution turned them black, so that in 1999 a
restoration programme was necessary to rediscover the architect's intention. In this picture
from 1911 the freshness remains and the full impact of the design can be appreciated.

The Old Bailey, London's central criminal court, stands on the site of the old Newgate Prison. It was the scene of numerous public executions in the eighteenth and nineteenth centuries following the removal of the gallows from Tyburn. The last took place in May 1868, barely fifty years before this photograph was taken. The name goes back to antiquity and refers to an enclosure that was part of the city walls between Ludgate and Newgate from Roman times.

Middle Temple in the first decade of the twentieth century. Its twelfth-century founders, the Templars, according to their own publicity, never dressed gaily and washed but seldom. Shaggy by reason of their uncombed hair, they were also begrimed with dust and swarthy from the weight of their armour and the heat of the sun. With this in mind, the injunction that formed part of their oath to 'shun feminine kisses, whether from widow, virgin, mother, sister, aunt or any other woman' seems somewhat extraneous.

Opposite: The Temple takes its name from the Knights Templar, who built their original round church in the twelfth century. The Master of the Temple at that time was Richard de Hastings. At first the Templars were considered soldiers of the church and were given their distinctive red-cross-emblazoned white mantles by Popes Honorius and Eugenius II. Pope Alexander III further granted them immunity from national jurisdictions. Later it became clear that they had what the church considered heretical beliefs and practices and they were banished, and their property made over to the Knights Hospitaller. They gave some of it away to Robert Blom – a man who had acted as a messenger for them in their dealings with the outside world – who built houses there and let them to 'a body of lawyers'. More than 700 years later The Temple is still the home of London's legal practitioners.

Demonstrations in London are neither a rare nor a recent phenomenon. When this photograph was taken, in 1909, the Suffragettes were making the news, marching through Trafalgar Square and the West End and selling work to support their cause at the Prince's skating-rink in Knightsbridge.

A view of Trafalgar Square in the early 1970s. The church of St Martin-in-the-Fields has held on to that name from the time when it was on the edge of the royal bit of London, with only fields beyond it.

Opposite: This is Trafalgar Square in the 1950s. Originally part of the Charing Cross area, the land was laid out as a memorial to the battle in 1829, but work didn't start on Nelson's Column until ten years later. A number of houses, streets and alleyways were removed in its creation, including chunks of St Martin's Lane, which now begins at house number 28 as a consequence.

The present church of St Martin-in-the-Fields dates from 1726, but the earliest on the site is recorded in 1222. These two pictures of it were taken in the 1930s.

The National Collection was begun in 1824 with the purchase, for £57,000, of
thirty-eight pictures belonging to the banker John Julius Angerstein. They were initially
put on display to the public at Angerstein's house in Pall Mall. The intention from the
beginning was that the exhibition would be free and easily available to the people of
London, rich and poor alike. When it outgrew its original location, a new building was
created at the 'crossroads of London' in Trafalgar Square. On the site of the old King's
Mews, it took six years to build and opened in 1838.

The Victoria and Albert Museum was founded in 1852. Originally known as the South Kensington Museum, it was renamed when the existing buildings were extended in 1899. Much of its exterior ornamentation was conceived by students at the Royal College of Art as a practical manifestation of the museum's stated mission to support and encourage excellence in art and design. The extended and redesigned buildings were finally completed in 1909 – an event commemorated by this postcard image.

Opposite: The basis for the Natural History Museum was the collection of Sir Hans Sloane – a major London landowner, physician and collector. He let the nation have it for a mere £20,000 with the stipulation that it be kept together and exhibited in London. It was first put on show in 1765 as part of the British Museum, which was then based at Montagu House in Bloomsbury. Fully a hundred years later Richard Owen, coiner of the term dinosaur and the then superintendent, enlisted Gladstone's help in persuading the government to give the collection a home of its own. A design competition was held in 1864 and the present 'cathedral to science' by Captain Francis Fowke was the winner. It opened in South Kensington's Cromwell Road in 1881.

Below: The Tate Gallery – now Tate Britain – stands on the site of the old Millbank prison, and was built to house the collection of (Tate & Lyle) sugar baron Sir Henry Tate. Tate didn't want his pictures to go to the National Gallery or any of the museums in South Kensington, so the authorities regarded his gift as a mixed blessing at first. Then an 'anonymous donor' came up with £80,000 for the construction of the gallery. Building commenced in 1893 and it was opened by the Prince of Wales (later Edward VII) in 1899. Two further extensions had been completed by the time of this photograph in 1910.

The British Museum gradually took over the site of Montagu House from about 1823, when that building had reached the limits of its potential for expansion. The main building was completed in 1845, the famous Reading Room in 1857. Various extensions to the original plan continued to be built throughout the twentieth century.

The free ferry at Woolwich was established in the fourteenth century. Seven hundred years on many hundreds of tons of vehicles and thousands of foot passengers a week continue to make the crossing here. This panoramic shot shows Woolwich in the early 1960s, looking across the river to North Woolwich, the Albert Docks and Silvertown, ten years before work began on the Thames Barrier. The forest of derricks in the distance to the right of the picture marks the site of the present London City Airport.

Below: Before the formation of the London Borough of Bexley, Woolwich – also at one time part of Kent – formed the easternmost boundary of London. It is unique among all the metropolitan boroughs in having land both sides of the river. Originally a fishing village, it grew in importance when a dockyard was established there in the sixteenth century. The Arsenal developed from the Brass Gun Foundry of 1716. The dockyard closed in 1869 and, after serving as a vital munitions factory during both world wars, the Arsenal was shut down in 1963 – about the time this photograph was taken.

The original Globe Theatre of Shakespearian fame stood a little way back from the river at Bankside – then part of Surrey – from 1599. The existence of a modern replica is due to the vision and determination of actor/director Sam Wanamaker. Born in Chicago in 1919, he moved to London during the period of the McCarthy 'witch hunts'. Sadly he died in London in 1993 before he could see his monumental project brought to fruition. These historic photographs show stages in the building of the new Globe between 1996 and 1998.

Hampstead Heath occupies one of London's highest points – Parliament Hill stands 319 feet above sea level. Its cosy name, which comes from homestead, or 'homely place', exactly suits the opinion in which it has been held by visitors since the tenth century. It was for many years (until the sixteenth century), however, the location of one of the Abbot of Westminster's gallows. Its name is also immortalised in the Cockney rhyming slang for 'teeth'. Still a peaceful spot, it is not now quite as bucolic as it was in 1911 when sheep, rather than a corporation mower, cropped the grass.

Church Row, Hampstead, in the 1960s. St John's church, a little further along, dates from 1745. Its copper spire was added in 1784. Among distinguished Hampstead residents buried there is the artist John Constable (d. 1837). Even fifty years ago parking was at such a premium that it was necessary for the Bedford van and some others to employ the crown of the road.

The Bull & Bush in Hampstead was originally built as a farmhouse in about 1645. It received its first licence to sell ale in 1721, but its real fame grew following its acquisition of a music licence in 1867. Florrie Forde's song is now one of the London sing-along standards, though it was written by an American and first published there as 'Under the Anheuser Busch'. These photographs afford wonderful 'before and after' views of it. The early picture dates from 1909 and shows the carthorses with their nosebags on while the carters went in for a quick one. In those days, before the imposition of restricted hours, it would have been open all day. Teas and dinners were on the menu and the terrace and gardens were a big attraction, as was the skittle alley. Its beers were supplied by Ind Coope then, just as they were at the time of the second picture – the late 1950s (right). Oddly, the signs in the later picture are more discreet. There has been some remodelling to the house, including the removal of what was probably a winch bay where the semi-circular façade has been added, but the main structure is little altered.

Stop in the name of the law! The London 'bobby' is now largely a thing of legend. In the past he was to be found at every junction, on every street corner, directing the traffic, guiding the lost and keeping time for the unwatched. The picture top left, from Judges' 'Arm of the law' series, shows an officer apparently about to unleash three Renault taxis on to Piccadilly Circus. In those times, when traffic travelled at widely differing speeds, three abreast seems to have been the norm in some parts of the capital. The other two pictures are from the late 1920s and seem to have been taken in Fleet Street, opposite the Punch Tavern. Formerly the Crown and Sugarloaf, this was renamed in honour of the magazine, which was conceived here in 1841. The images show the same crossing, although the man with the pedal-barrow and the flat cap is not the same. The second picture (above) was taken by Judges when it was realised that the first contravened restrictions on alcohol advertising. It's a safe bet the barrow showed the Whitbread lorry and the contractor's cart a clean pair of heels when advised by a signal from the officer to proceed with caution.

The furled sails and old mooring piles in these pictures from before the First World War
give St Paul's and the north bank something of the look of Venice. Traditions of a
Christian temple on this site at the top of Ludgate Hill go back way before Wren's
masterpiece or either of the previously known Norman and Saxon churches.
It is believed there was some sort of shrine here in the second century. Wren himself
found a tiny image of the Roman goddess Diana during his excavations.

The General Post Office in St Martins-le-Grand near St Paul's in 1909. Built in 1829 in classical style, with a 400 foot frontage, 70 feet of which was occupied by the grand portico, it nevertheless outgrew itself in a short time, necessitating the building of GPO North on the opposite side of the road.

This page and opposite: The symbol and heart of the city, these night shots of St Paul's
reveal much of its atmosphere and the majesty of its proportions.

LS4. LONDON. ST. PAUL'S CATHEDRAL.
THE CRYPT. ARTISTS' CORNER.

JUDGES

Artists' Corner at St Paul's, wrongly described as part of the crypt – the daylight
streaming through the window is a bit of a giveaway. This is actually the south transept.

Some interiors of the great cathedral taken by master photographer John Edwards in the 1970s.

ir Christopher Wren's omb in St Paul's is lain and unadorned. If you seek his nonument, look about ou,' it sagely advises. The same is not true of hat of Nelson, which s fittingly dramatic in oth style and location. The Admiral was uried here in 1806.

When the US Army Air Force chiefs brought up the idea of a memorial to those of their men who had fallen, towards the end of the Second World War, RAF Marshal Trenchard said that it was the duty of the British to provide such a monument. The Dean of St Paul's, Walter Matthews, suggested the cathedral as a fitting location. It was established at the extreme east end, where the sanctuary had suffered bomb damage, and was dedicated by HM Queen Elizabeth II in 1958.

Opposite: It took some time for traffic levels to build up again in the city after the Second World War, as can be seen in this picture of St Paul's and Ludgate Hill.

Mysterious goings on outside the New York Herald's offices in Fleet Street in 1909. Everyone's attention seems to be on some kind of incident occurring between the taxi and the second Putney bus. Some of the crowd with the straw boaters, the two police officers in the middle of the road, the man at the front of the first Putney bus and the police officer on the number 58 for Shoreditch have all seen something of which everyone else is unaware.

Westminster Abbey in 1909 with hansom cab. Like St Paul's it is believed that the abbey is built on the site of an ancient place of worship – in this case of the Roman god Apollo. The Dean of St Paul's thought his opposite number was jumping on the bandwagon when this suggestion came to light. 'The Dean of Westminster must produce an image of Apollo as like that of the Belvedere as this [the one at St Paul's] to the Diana of the Louvre, before he can fairly compete with us for the antiquity of heathen worship,' he wrote.

Opposite: Twelve and a half million handmade bricks were used in the construction of Westminster Cathedral, completed in 1903. In 1925, at about the time this photograph was taken, a woman threw herself and her three children from the top of the campanile, causing it to be closed until a high railing could be added. The Byzantine building, designed by J.F. Bentley, incorporates columns of the same marble used by Justinian for St Sophia in Constantinople.

The front of Westminster Abbey from Tothill Street in the 1930s, complete with the latest invention of then Minister of Transport, Leslie Hore-Belisha – London's, and the world's, first flashing light pedestrian crossings, the Belisha Beacons.

The interior of the abbey. The north ambulatory in about 1920 and the choir a decade or so later.

Henry VII's chapel was completed in 1519 and has long been regarded by many as the finest existing example of Tudor vaulted architecture.

The Coronation Chair was made on the order of Edward I when the legendary Stone of Scone was brought to London from Dunbar in 1296.

Holborn Viaduct cost over £2 million to build and was opened by Queen Victoria in November 1869. This photograph, taken in Farringdon Street in 1909, shows the 107-foot-long iron bridge, which stands roughly where Holborn Bridge crossed the old Fleet River.

This is the area known as Holborn Bar, so named because it marked the point where a toll had to be paid to enter the city – commemorated by the granite pillars. The Bar escaped the Great Fire of 1666 without damage, but only these glorious half-timbered houses escaped the ravages of later neglect and planning.

Dedicated to St Margaret of Antioch, a little-known saint whose cult was very popular in the middle ages, the church of St Margaret's Westminster was built largely as somewhere for the public to go where they would cease to bother the monks in Westminster Abbey next door. Although much restored, it retains much of the ancient character dating from its rebuilding and reconsecration in the sixteenth century.

The timeless and unmistakable outline of Barry's Houses of Parliament, taken from across the river in around 1911. Below we see Parliament in the mid-1960s, with the statue of Jan Smuts, looking for all the world as if he is ice-skating.

A unique record of night time in old Westminster in the 1920s – a horse-drawn bus waits in the pool of gas light.

A little way north from St Paul's, Smithfield was (and is) London's meat market. Established in 1614, it originally dealt in livestock. In 1869 the new meat hall was built. The largest meat market in the world, it contains 15 miles of meat hanging rails.

The Charing Cross was erected in
memory of Queen Eleanor
(d. 1290), but there was a place
called Charing here before that time,
its name probably derived from the
making of charcoal.

Very many years ago Covent Garden was the garden of the Westminster convent. For three hundred years it was the London market for flowers, fruit and vegetables. Finally it outgrew its traditional location and a new site was opened at Nine Elms in 1974. During the eighteenth century it was a rather sleazy area, the equivalent of a modern red-light district, with bawdy houses and communal Turkish baths – or hammams.

Ludgate Hill is the continuation of Fleet Street in the direction of St Paul's via Ludgate Circus. The name refers to one of the older gates in the city walls and probably means 'back gate'. These night time shots were taken in 1924.

St James's Park around the time of the First World War. The best part of 100 acres, it was set aside by Henry VIII as an open space and continued in a fairly wild condition until James I had it laid out and set up a zoo there. The lake is known as Rosamund's Pond.

St James's Palace was built on the site of a hospital for female lepers. It was built by Henry VIII in 1533 and finally became the home of the Lord Chamberlain's office. The James in question was a bishop of Jerusalem.

A very Edwardian scene in Waterlow Park, Highgate, in 1909. The park was the gift of Sir Sidney Waterlow in 1889. Lauderdale House here was built in the 1660s. Charles II left Nell Gwynne in residence while he was away in Scotland. By the middle of the twentieth century it had been converted into the park's tea rooms.

Probably Highgate Cemetery's most famous 'resident', Karl Marx. Others include Radclyffe Hall and John Galsworthy.

Above: Highgate Hill has been a desirable area of London for centuries – its elevated position rendering it free from most of the pollutions and contagions of the lower streets. The roadway was not built until the fourteenth century, so the gate was not the busiest entrance to London before that time. This picture dates from about 1971.

Broadcasting House shortly after its completion in 1931. The BBC had by this time more than outgrown its premises in Savoy Hill. These purpose-built studios began broadcasting in 1932 and continue to be the home of BBC Radio to this day.

Above: The world's first public broadcast television service came on the air in 1936. BBC TV was based at Alexandra Palace until the mammoth new Television Centre in Wood Lane was built in the late 1950s.

Thomas Carlyle's House at 5 (later 24) Cheyne Row, Chelsea, in the 1930s. Scottish-born essayist and historian Carlyle died here in 1881.

The painter James McNeill Whistler commissioned the design of The White House in Tite Street, off Chelsea Embankment, in 1877, from the architect E.W. Godwin. Whistler died on 17 July 1903.

Below: Chelsea probably owes its origins to a former chalk wharf – its name deriving from the same root as calcium. This picture, taken in the 1930s, provides a record of the parish church, most of which was destroyed by a bomb in 1941.

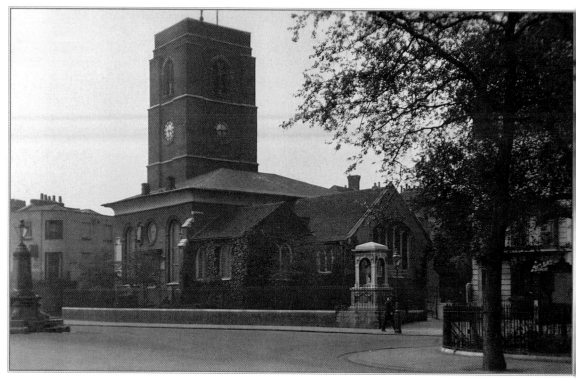

The heart of London's financial district. Here are the Bank of England and The Royal
Exchange. The picture above was taken from the Exchange in 1909, when it was still a
meeting place for brokers dealing in foreign bills. This all came to an end in 1921 and
Lloyd's quit the building in 1928, not long before the second photograph was taken,
when it passed to Royal Exchange Assurance.

Above: Waterloo Place in about 1920. The Athenaeum Club was established here in 1823 and the building on the left of this picture was the London headquarters of what was then the Italian State Railway.

The Monument commemorating the Great Fire of London in 1666. For many years it was believed that Wren was its designer, but he had gone a bit overboard with golden flames and a big phoenix on the top, so the more restrained plan from City Surveyor Robert Hooke was chosen instead.

Holden's building for the University of London was built with the aid of a grant from the Rockefeller Foundation. Although occupied here in the 1930s, it was not completed until after the Second World War. The university headquarters later moved to Egham and Richmond, and this building was taken over by the Ministry of Education.

The Mansion House was the first official residence of the Mayors of London. It was
built in 1752. Before that the mayors were expected to host civic functions in their own
houses, or at rented inns.

All maritime movements were monitored by the Port of London Authority from this
wonderfully ornate building from its opening in 1922, commemorated by this
photograph. Sixty years on there are plans afoot to turn it into a hotel, all its former
business having been transferred elsewhere.

Standing in Cheapside, about midway between St Paul's and the Bank of England,
St Mary-le-Bow was St Mary's at the 'arch' in its earliest records. Bow and arch are
synonymous – and bow sounds remarkably like 'pont', when pronounced in Norman
French. It is thought that it stands on what was once part of Watling Street and occupies
the site of an earlier shrine. There has been a Christian church here since 1081.

The laying out of Regent's Park in what had been Marylebone Fields took place between 1812 and 1838. Both Nash and Decimus Burton were involved in its design.

This Roman bastion in the churchyard of St Giles's, Cripplegate, is a remnant of the 'barbican' which, two thousand years on, gives its name to this part of London and the new developments nearby. The church itself survived the Great Fire of 1666.

St Bride's church is actually dedicated to the Irish Saint Bridget. The existence of such a church is recorded as far back as 1222. Samuel Pepys was baptised there in 1633. The present building with its singular pagoda-like steeple is the work of Wren, the original having been lost in the fire of 1666. Still the third highest ecclesiastical building in London (after St Paul's and Westminster cathedrals), at 226 feet, it is 8 feet shorter than intended, following a lightning strike in 1764.

When he first came to London Samuel (later Doctor) Johnson worked in the room
above St John's Gate in Clerkenwell. He also dined there, behind a screen, since he was
considered too disreputable of appearance to be observed by his fellow diners.
Originally the entrance to the Priory of St John of Jerusalem, it later (1877) became the
appropriate headquarters for the St John's Ambulance Association.

The first Lambeth Bridge was a cheapjack suspension affair opened in 1862. It was regarded as such an eyesore by Lambeth Palace that they demanded – and won – compensation. The presence of Horseferry Road as a continuation of the road to the north of the bridge is an indicator of the previous means of crossing at this point. Seen here is the bright new bridge opened in 1932 – three years after the demolition of the old.

Wyatt's statue of the 'grand old' Duke of York in a rather countrified-looking Carlton Gardens in around 1910. The view from it was considered altogether preferable to the view of it, its column being both disproportionately tall and thick. For the first years after its opening in 1833, it was mainly known for the number of people who chose to jump off it.

Built in 1567, the Old Curiosity Shop in Portsmouth Street by Lincoln's Inn probably owes its continued existence to Dickens's novel. This photograph was taken in 1910.

Coach drivers on the old A2 used to put it about that Blackheath got its name because it was a burial place for plague victims. The truth is that it was always a dark-coloured heath. Wat Tyler and his men camped here in 1381 and the people of London welcomed Henry V back here from his victory at Agincourt in 1415. All Saints' church was completed with the addition of a porch in 1899. Built from Kentish ragstone, it was designed by Benjamin Ferrey.

The Pagoda at Kew Gardens in the 1930s. Designed by William Chambers, architect to George III's mother, the Dowager Princess of Wales, it was completed – along with the Orangery – in the early 1760s.

A late bus. The streetlights were gas and those on the bus itself probably paraffin-fuelled.

The newsboy. Not just an unmistakable sight for many decades, one of the traditional sounds of London was the news vendors shouting their unique – and often incomprehensible – news headlines to passers-by.

Outside the Gaiety Theatre in 1924. The first Gaiety in The Aldwych was built in 1864 and known as the Strand Music Hall. This palatial affair replaced it in 1903, but was demolished in 1957.

'All hot.' This was the cry of the roast chestnut vendors, whose handcarts and braziers contributed to the sights, sounds and aromas of old London for generations. A victim of corporate and franchised fast food, they have gone the way of much that made the capital special.

In this picture of Tottenham Court Road in 1924, the underground station already has the illuminated London Transport logo. In those days the next stop on the Central Line to St Paul's (then called Post Office) was British Museum. Removed from the maps in 1932, this is one of about forty abandoned underground stations in London – many of whose walls still display contemporary posters.

The pavements of Regent Street have rarely ceased to bustle – as in this night time photograph. Cab, anyone?

The shoeblack. Shoeblacks were still a common feature of London in the 1960s, though this one dates from half a century earlier. The advent of Padawax and the decline of the shiny shoe since then makes this thickly atmospheric image all the more historical.

JUDGES POSTCARDS
A brief history

There is every chance that the postcard you send home from your holiday started life in Sussex. Since 1902 Hastings has been the home of Judges, one of Britain's leading publishers of quality picture postcards.

When Fred Judge arrived in Hastings in 1902 he could have had little idea of the worldwide impact he was to make on the business of postcard publishing. But Fred was a master with a camera and a natural entrepreneur. Fred Judge was born in Yorkshire in 1872. Photography was always his real interest, and it was while visiting Sussex in 1902 that he made the decision to give up engineering for a career as a photographer.

Fred and his brother Thomas purchased an existing business in Hastings and set up as photographers and photographic dealers under the name of Judge's Photo Stores. Although the idea of sending an illustrated card through the post was not new (the first having appeared towards the end of the nineteenth century) Fred made his mark by setting himself extremely high artistic standards. At first he concentrated on local scenes and activities. Having taken his pictures he would go straight back to the darkroom to make them into postcards – often for sale within a few hours; and the quality of his work was such that passers by would gather outside the shop window for a sight of his latest work.

Technically stunning, and using all the latest photographic technology, Fred's pictures won over 100 medals, and one-man exhibitions of his work were held in London, Washington, New York and Tokyo.

Back in Hastings the business was expanding, necessitating moves to bigger and better premises, culminating in the move in 1927 to the purpose-built factory that the company occupies to this day. Although the building has been developed and extended, the Italianate façade remains a famous landmark on the A259 coast road.

Fred Judge died in February 1950 at the age of 78, having built up an internationally respected company. The business was sold to another Judges photographer, who introduced lithographic colour printing. Then in 1984 Judges became a real family concern once again when Bernard and Jan Wolford took over. It became even more of a family business when their son Graeme, now managing director, joined, followed by Trevor, now sales director. The present management can truly be said to be building on the foundations laid by Fred Judge over ninety years ago.

Judges Postcards Ltd, 176 Bexhill Road, St Leonards on Sea,
East Sussex, TN38 8BN
Tel: 01424 420919; Fax: 01424 438538
www.judges.co.uk